Complaining or Contented?

Janet Goodall

Gilead Books Publishing
www.GileadBooksPublishing.com

First published in Great Britain in 2020

2 4 6 8 10 9 7 5 3 1

Copyright © Janet Goodall 2020

British Library Cataloguing-in-Publication Data:
A catalogue record for this book is available from the British Library.

ISBN-13: 978-1-8381828-0-9

All rights reserved.
No part of this publication may be reproduced, stored in a retrieval system or transmitted in any form or by any means, electronic, mechanical, photocopying, recording or otherwise, without the prior permission of the publisher.

Unless stated otherwise, scriptures are taken from The Holy Bible, New Inter-national Version®, NIV® Copyright © 1973, 1978, 1984, 2011 by Biblica, Inc.
® Used by permission. All rights reserved worldwide.

For Sue and Stuart Cooke for all their uncomplaining care in so many ways, and for Valerie MacKay, one of the most contented women I know.

Contents

	Introduction	6
1.	It's all your fault	10
2.	I can't manage that	18
3.	Why are we waiting?	26
4.	Since you ask…	37
5.	Nobody talks to me	44
6.	Is anybody there?	52
7.	I'm so scared	60
8.	Surely church people don't complain	71
9.	Sweet contentment despite the trials	81
10.	God's purposes are always good	89
11.	To God be the glory	101

Acknowledgements

Chris Hayes of Gilead Books kindly accepted this little book for publication at the very stressful time of the Covid-19 pandemic, and I thank him most sincerely.

Thanks, too, to David Burton for his punctilious editing despite an already demanding schedule.

I am very grateful to Dr Valerie MacKay for taking time to read and comment so helpfully on the manuscript.

Ken and Jackie Hulme helped with the final stage of preparation for the press and I am most grateful to them.

Others have helpfully read and commented on parts of the manuscript whilst some have unwittingly prompted my thoughts on both aspects of the title. I am indebted to you all.

Introduction

Years ago I was in Australia, one of five intrepid explorers who were about to embark on a camping trip from the centre of that vast country to its northern coast. A fellow traveller greeted me by asking, 'Are you a Pom?'

I admitted to being British, but was rather put out by his next question – 'Are you a *whinging* Pom?'

I learned then that the word indicated peevish complaining, and was regarded as an attitude typical of my compatriots. Ouch!

There are, of course, complaints that are not peevish. When doctors ask, 'What's the problem?' they expect to hear some complaints. Public-spirited individuals complain to the authorities about the state of the roads, the numbers of homeless, certain public policies and much more. These do not classify as 'whinging', but this is the sort of complaining which we'll be considering in this book. It is the element of self-pity in a complaint that identifies it as whinging or grumbling. I want to highlight some common whinges, as indicated in the chapter titles, but then point to a different way of dealing with genuine complaints.

It is easy to complain, and even easier to whinge, but as Christians we have clear instructions to approach our hardships and irritations in a much better way, whilst not denying them. Our aim should be to encourage others and give glory to God, and this book is a humble attempt to explore that different way.

The question in the title – 'Complaining or contented?' – was already on my mind when a series of vexations arose in my life which ensured that I could not take a lofty position. I found myself complaining about the various trials of a single day to three separate visitors before I caught myself at it and was reminded afresh that I constantly need to face the challenge of not 'whinging' as much as any reader might. We are all in this together.

It's our common experience to face problems – to embark on frustrating phone-calls, hear of a change of plan that inconveniently affects fixtures in the diary, cope with interruptions that ruin our intended programme for the day or, outside the home, suffer inconsiderate drivers who push in on our right of way. Hopes of keeping calm give way to frustration, which can explode into angry words or deeds, and tell the watching world that all is not well. Mothers of small children are sometimes mortified to hear their children repeat their own irritable comments. We all experience testing times, and too often fail the test.

Throughout the Bible we meet characters whose reactions to challenge were as negative as ours can be. Yet we also find the instruction, 'do not grumble',[1] and Paul's serene statement (from prison!) that 'I have learned the secret of being content in any and every situation'.[2]

Was Paul's an open secret? This is what we are about to explore. At the same time, we'll consider some real-life experiences in which the natural first reaction was

---

[1] 1 Corinthians 10:10
[2] Philippians 4:12

to complain. These stories may ring a few bells, but hopefully also point to that better way.

1. It's all your fault

It started in the Garden of Eden.

The Lord God had created a wonderful world, including this beautiful garden. Here he enjoyed the company of a human couple who represented the pinnacle of his creativity. Sadly their harmony was spoiled when the man, Adam, and his wife, Eve, were tempted to disobey the Lord God.

God had told Adam that he could enjoy all the fruit growing in the garden except that from two particular trees. Despite the fruit of those trees looking very attractive, there would be serious consequences should Adam ignore the warning, which he would doubtless have shared with Eve.

For a time, all went well. They delighted in the fauna and flora around them, and had the amazing joy of personal visits from the Lord himself in the cool of the evening. Then, one dreadful day, everything changed.

God's sworn enemy slithered into the garden and challenged the ban on the two fruit trees. He persuaded the woman to take a sample of fruit from one of them, saying that it would show her the difference between right and wrong. She thought it looked delicious, took a bite, and enjoyed it so much that she persuaded Adam to try some too.

The whole sad story is told in Genesis 3, and the end result was the expulsion from Eden of the unhappy couple. For our purposes here, I want to think about the wrangling that went on when the Lord arrived on the scene and their disobedience was exposed.

The man said, 'The woman you put here with me – she gave me some fruit from the tree, and I ate it.' In response, the woman said, 'The snake deceived me and I ate.'[3] Neither of them took the blame for their actions; in fact, Adam hinted that in the end it was the

[3] Genesis 3:12-13

Lord's fault for having given him such an untrustworthy partner! In turn, Eve blamed the one who had deceived her. Both of them complained that they had been led astray. It was not their fault.

Shelving responsibility

What a familiar strategy this is. Even young children, caught in some wrongdoing, might protest that 'it wasn't me', and complain that 'it's not fair' if accusations persist. Responsibility for a broken toy can be offloaded onto a boisterous playmate, or even the dog, rather than owning up to it.

This tendency continues into adulthood. How often have we heard someone in public life claim to have 'done nothing wrong' when they're justifiably accused of some immoral activity, and complain that their accusers are ganging up on them. The same attitude shows up everywhere, down to the behaviour of drivers who show road rage towards another's supposedly bad driving with no admission of their own liability.

Such complaints and resentments can smoulder on, to be shared with a sympathetic circle until they become a major topic of conversation and gossip, stirring up more discontent. On the grand scale, at times this can even escalate into an outbreak of dangerous hostility.

This is illustrated by a dark episode in the life of King David.[4] He admired, coveted and took Bathsheba, another man's wife, whilst her husband, Uriah, was away fighting on his king's behalf. When she became pregnant, David hatched a plot to make it seem that Uriah was the baby's father; but the scheme failed. How David must have complained about this before thinking up an even worse idea. He gave orders to his army commander that in the next battle he was to put this loyal soldier out in front where the fighting was fiercest, then withdraw from him. Uriah was killed, and David quickly married his widow – an altogether shameful sequence of behaviour. It took a prophet's rebuke for the adulterous royal murderer to face up to his sin.

Yet out of that sordid episode came Psalm 51, a psalm of confession and contrition, where David pleads with God to be cleansed from the stain of sin, and for the renewal of a right spirit within him. This was the only way to find forgiveness and recover contentment in

---

[4] 2 Samuel 11:1-27

'the joy of salvation'. His 'broken and contrite heart' would be made right again with his God – but David still had to live with the consequences of his actions.

God made me like this

Adam was not the only one to imply that it was God's fault when things did not go well for him. In his case it was disobedience that had clearly sent things awry, while others assert that God is completely to blame for harm that can come from their personality traits or dependencies (such as obsessive behaviour or drug and alcohol abuse). Suggesting that God should be held responsible for such behaviour ignores the evidence that some very fundamental things about us are shaped by external factors, such as upbringing, as much as being innate. Having designed us to live in a network of caring relationships, first with him and also with others,[5] it is the effect on those others that often highlights where our traits are used to excuse our sins. Too often both parties just express their complaints, instead of seeking to be in better relationships with one another.

---

[5] Matthew 22:37-39

If that fails, help is at hand for such problems, including sympathetic counselling. Sometimes the troublesome tendencies can be turned to good use. An obsessional person can, with help, learn to use that aspect of their personality in, say, accountancy or administration, where focused attention to detail matters immensely. (This is not to say that all accountants or administrators have personality problems!) At the same time, obsessional people should seek to curb the tendency to pursue every possible side avenue, or define every matter of detail, where it burdens others unnecessarily.

We need to remember that God gave us all freedom to choose by the exercise of our will and, if we ask him, wills can be directed and fortified by his Holy Spirit.[6] Some problems may seem insuperable, because part of the affliction is limited willpower, and this is the time for 'neighbours' to decide to show their love by supporting affected people, persistently showing friendship rather than complaining about them.

[6] Romans 8:5-11

Finding contentment

What about us? What do we grumble about? Our complaints may not be nearly as momentous as the complaints of others, but the Bible warns us against grumblers and fault-finders[7] – we are specifically instructed not to be like them.[8] Yet a cursory glance through the Psalms reveals how the psalmists frequently give free rein to their different woes.

The key difference – and the thing we need to learn – is expressed by David: 'Hear me, O God, as I voice my complaint.'[9] While we tend to voice our complaints to anyone who is prepared to listen, the safest person with whom to share them – one who will spread them no further – is our loving God.

'Take it to the Lord in prayer' is an old hymn with an up-to-date message. It is through his loving forgiveness and renewal, as we tell him all about it and confess where we have been in error, that we find contentment. There is no need to offload onto anyone else – but, since we are still human, it's likely that we'll unburden ourselves to a special friend. Better still

[7] Jude:16
[8] James 5:9
[9] Psalm 64:1

would be to find a prayer partner and pray about the difficulty together. A problem shared becomes so much less of a problem when it is handed over to our almighty God.

2. I can't manage that

From infancy onwards we learn by surmounting things which at first seemed beyond our capability. For a toddler it could just be a flight of stairs, or for a schoolchild perhaps mental arithmetic, followed by increasingly tough examinations, until in early adulthood comes the first day in a new job. I remember being appointed to a more senior medical post than I'd held before, and having my many new duties and commitments explained to me by the departing doctor. My first thought was, 'I'll never manage to do all that!' Then it dawned on me that I would be working through my new agenda one day at a time, not doing it all at once – and that experienced advice was on hand. This is also true of other tasks which, at first, we may complain will overwhelm us.

In contrast, some employers expect their workforce to produce unreasonably high output with inadequate pay. Complaints to the management about what feels like slave labour risk losing the job, although much muttering will continue on the shop floor. This was the situation of the Israelites in Egypt, where they were indeed being treated as slaves, and groaning under severe oppression. They had started out as God's chosen people, so why had he allowed them to come to this?

The Lord heard their cries, saw their misery, and made a plan of action. In Exodus 5 we read how God sent Moses and Aaron to approach Pharaoh on the Israelites' behalf. They asked him to release the Israelites – who were the major part of his workforce – to attend a festival. The request was angrily turned down, and a backlash was imposed on the workers, who would now be expected to produce the same tally of bricks as before, whilst finding their own straw with which to make them. They bitterly complained about this injustice to Moses and Aaron. Seven chapters and ten plagues later, Pharaoh finally let them go. The plagues had been awful – the last plague had deprived the Egyptians of their firstborn sons but spared the Israelites, who celebrated with a special Passover meal before being led out from Egypt to head for the Promised Land of Canaan.

Growth in maturity

When the Lord had first called him to this, Moses too had complained. Just listen to him:

> 'Who am I that I should go to Pharaoh...?'[10]
>
> 'What if they (the Israelites) do not believe me...?'[11]
>
> 'Pardon your servant, Lord. I have never been eloquent...I am slow of speech and tongue.'[12]
>
> 'Pardon your servant, Lord. Please send someone else.'[13]

The Lord had already promised to be with Moses and tell him what to say, so he was justifiably angry at this reluctant reaction. Although God responded by enlisting Aaron to do the talking, Moses was not let off the hook – he still had to tell his brother what to say. Yet in the end the Lord made Moses the leader when

---

[10] Exodus 3:11
[11] Exodus 4:1
[12] Exodus 4:10
[13] Exodus 4:13

the whole company of Israelites escaped from Egypt and crossed the Red Sea. Later Moses would be described as uniquely humble.[14] He received a glowing testimonial from the Lord, emphasising his faithfulness within the close relationship they eventually shared.[15] Because the people repeatedly complained about the hardships of the journey, Moses had constantly needed to turn to his Lord for wisdom. At one point the community even threatened to stone him, wrongly complaining that he was expecting them to do more than had been expected of them when they were slaves in Egypt. Moses had a lot to bear, but he even pleaded for his people when the Lord threatened to wipe them out for their disobedience.[16]

The road to maturity is usually an obstacle course, but those who trust in God are assured that he is an ever-present help in trouble.[17] To experience the truth of this promise is to develop a closer relationship with him, as Moses shows us. From the unwilling instrument he had been at the start of his ministry, Moses came to learn obedience by depending

[14] Numbers 12:3
[15] Numbers 12:6-8
[16] Exodus 32:9-13
[17] Psalm 46:1

completely on his Lord. Their relationship became so close that they spoke face to face, and Moses' countenance shone with reflected glory.[18]

Hindrance or help?

When they reached Mount Sinai, the Lord spoke powerfully to the Israelites. He gave them the Ten Commandments, and warned them against any disobedience. Moses then disappeared up the mountain to receive further instructions, and was away for so long that rebellion broke out in the camp. The people enlisted Aaron's aid to make a golden calf to be their new god. Moses returned and, very shocked, executed the Lord's order of severe punishment. The tragedy unfolds in Exodus 32.

Later in the journey, Moses sent out spies to report on what they could find in Canaan. All but two, Caleb and Joshua, foresaw fierce opposition from the powerful inhabitants of what was very desirable territory. What they saw was too much for them – they feared that the cost of further invasion would be too high, and failed to trust that the Lord who had brought them so far would give them the victory anticipated by Caleb and

---

[18] Exodus 34:29-35

Joshua. Because of this lack of faith, none of the spies survived the Exodus but those two. The rest gradually died off during the further wanderings the Lord imposed on the Israelites as a result of their fearfulness. The journey from Sinai to Canaan could normally have taken eleven days, but the people's repeated complaints and disobedience extended it to forty years!

The end result of complaining

During those forty years of wandering, the words groaning, grumbling, murmuring and complaining repeatedly crop up in the story. First the Israelites disdained the daily basic food the Lord provided. They then complained of thirst, a need which God miraculously met. Grumbling had begun only three days into their march, and continued at intervals throughout it. Although their main target was Moses, they were really murmuring against the Lord, despite owing their liberation to him. Yet after that the Lord went ahead of them day and night, making their way plain with signposts of cloud and fire – and still their ingratitude was boundless, despite the Lord's clear warning:

'How long will this wicked community grumble against me? I have heard the complaints of these grumbling Israelites...In this wilderness your bodies will fall...'[19]

Complaints against Jesus himself

Centuries later that story found echoes during Jesus' ministry on earth. Whereas many social outcasts and others followed Jesus and marvelled at his teaching, we read that the Pharisees and teachers of the law 'muttered' criticism about him.[20] They even sneered at him.[21] Other Jews grumbled when they understood neither his reference to himself as nourishing spiritual bread, nor his statement that he was sent by his heavenly Father. They murmured against his claim to belong to more than just a human family when they only knew him as the son of Joseph the carpenter – and Jesus told them to 'stop grumbling'.[22] Many of Jesus' disciples heard this exchange, and began to grumble themselves. When he fully explained the inner meaning of the discussion to these supposed followers

---

[19] Numbers 14:27-29
[20] Luke 15:1-2
[21] Luke 16:14
[22] John 6:41-43

of his, some of them turned back and left him.[23] Jesus knew that some would even go on to betray him, in particular Judas, who would eventually be so full of remorse that he took his own life.[24] Grumbling can have drastic consequences.

Yet if only Jesus' followers had understood and accepted his teaching, they would have found contentment and rest for their souls[25] – and so may we.

[23] John 6:60-66
[24] Matthew 27:3-5
[25] Matthew 11:29

3. Why are we waiting?

Every driver knows about waiting, either at traffic lights or in a traffic jam. Expectant mothers await their anticipated date of delivery. Small children 'can't wait' for Christmas or their next birthday. Students wait apprehensively for examination results, lovers wait for a phone-call or message from their beloved, commuters wait for a delayed train, long lines of customers wait for their turn at the shop counter, insomniacs wait for dawn, relatives of a dying dear one wait for the end, and the writer waits for inspiration. Some of those who wait complain louder than others.

In the developing world, most waiting is for very different reasons. Our screens show us queues snaking into the distance as desperate people wait for food aid to be unloaded, or as they line up with tin mugs and plastic containers for their turn at a new well. Rural farmers (and others) long for rain to fall on their parched fields, while roughly-bandaged victims of conflict wait for medical aid and combatants wait for a ceasefire. Wherever we live, from start to finish, our lives hold experiences of waiting.

How are we waiting?

News reporters sometimes approach travellers whose plane has been cancelled, or whose train has been delayed. Those interviewed are either frustrated or philosophical, more often the former. Air passengers complain of a holiday spoiled before it started, of failed connections and important missed events, and the associated inconvenience to friends who have been waiting at the airport to greet them. Commuters complain of being late for work – *again* – and the risk of being fired if this keeps happening regardless of how notoriously the trains are delayed. Airports and station platforms sometimes seem to seethe with discontented people, amongst whom the occasional uncomplaining travellers stand out as they quietly go with the flow. In which group would we – or do we – find ourselves?

In the context of healthcare, waiting in vain for an unlikely recovery might prove too much for a patient's relatives. One bereaved father spoke of how he had nearly punched the doctor who told him that his son had died after years of illness. He even shook the dead body in his disbelief, trying to bring his boy back to life. Violence towards health professionals is rising, thanks to drug and alcohol abuse by ungrateful clients. Teachers complain of rebellious pupils, some of whom carry knives. As professionals like these wait to start the day's work, they might be excused for complaining that things are no longer as they used to be.

An alternative to complaining

We have perhaps shared such frustrations at times, but none of us will ever undergo the catalogue of problems Paul spells out in his second letter to the Corinthians. We read how he encountered circumstances which demanded great endurance, 'in troubles, hardships and distresses; in beatings, imprisonments and riots; in hard work, sleepless nights and hunger; *in purity, understanding, patience and kindness; in the Holy Spirit and in sincere love; in truthful speech and in the power of God; with weapons of righteousness in the right hand and in the left;* through glory and dishonour, bad report and good report; genuine, yet regarded as imposters; known, yet regarded as unknown; dying, and yet we live on; beaten and yet not killed; sorrowful, yet always rejoicing; poor, yet making many rich; having nothing and yet possessing everything.'[26]

The italics are mine, but they mark a surprising departure from the rest of his list, with echoes of the fruit of the Holy Spirit as described for the Galatians[27] and the spiritual armour spelt out for the Ephesians.[28] When speaking objectively of his many difficulties, Paul evidently relied on the Holy Spirit's fruit of patience rather than gratifying his natural frustration. The armour of God enabled him to overcome, without complaint, what were in reality assaults from the enemy of his soul. We'll think again about some of these trials in chapter 8.

Yet there was a time when an unspecified 'thorn in the flesh' so troubled Paul that he pleaded with the Lord to take it away. Did he complain about it? If so, the Lord's answer is one we can apply to our lesser trials.

---

[26] 2 Corinthians 6:4-10
[27] Galatians 5:17,22-23
[28] Ephesians 6:10-17

'My grace is sufficient for you, for my power is made perfect in weakness.'[29]

Engage the mind before opening the mouth

Paul said that he had *learned* to be content.[30] There has only ever been one apostle Paul, but as we follow his example we will find the same Spirit of Jesus that he did, ready to come to our rescue when we're about to express our irritation. We are being taught by the same Master but, as with any other lesson, the pupil must be ready to listen attentively and then act on the instruction. There are special classes for slow learners. Most of us need to attend them and are likely to be given repeated opportunities for learning more patience. James tells us that our words have an influence, either for good or ill.[31] All too often, our willpower fails to bridle an impatient and complaining tongue – but if we catch ourselves in time and send up a quick SOS prayer instead, we will find the Holy Spirit ever-ready to provide the patience and self-control we need at that moment.

---

[29] 2 Corinthians 12:9
[30] Philippians 4:12
[31] James 3:1-12

Who hears our complaints?

The Psalms hold many songs of woe, but the psalmists also acknowledge the safe refuge that is to be found in God.[32] [33] He is the first one they call to as they pour out their troubles.[34] [35] An old hymn tells us that if we have trials and temptations we should take them to the Lord in prayer, for he is the proper first port of call. We may also find a prayer partner to share the burden, in this way being helped to reduce the pressure we're feeling. Instead of airing our frustrations with all around us, it can be a relief to find a sympathetic ear – and none better than that of our constantly attentive heavenly counsellor.

From his many testing experiences David had proved this resource to be true. He could say, 'I waited patiently for the Lord; he turned to me and heard my cry.'[36]

---

[32] Psalm 37:4
[33] Psalm 46:1
[34] Psalm 64:1
[35] Psalm 145:18-19
[36] Psalm 40:1

Waiting patiently?

There are much greater troubles than ours in the world, which should put our own into perspective. When I worked in Uganda as a paediatrician I was shocked to see so many desperately sick children. On my very first ward-round I saw a little girl with kwashiorkor, a severe form of malnutrition which is commoner in girls, because boys are allowed to roam around and pick up tit-bits, whereas girls are usually not given that freedom. The condition is marked by generalised swelling of the body, but what struck me forcibly about this child was her air of profound misery. She avoided eye contact and turned her head away from any friendly overtures. I learned that the condition commonly arose in that culture when a previously breastfed infant was abruptly weaned, often by being sent to a different home altogether. There, she would wait in vain to see her mother again, with the resultant depression taking away her appetite. Emotional deprivation accompanied the physical malnutrition—yet should her mother eventually return, hope deferred had made the child's heart faint and unresponsive, even to her. The wound had gone too deep for a quick recovery. Her whole demeanour was a complaint without words.

Why then should David say in contrast, 'I have calmed and quieted myself; I am like a weaned child with its mother'?[37] The secret of his contentment lay in the sustained relationship with the one who had always loved him and would never send him away or abandon him, who had supplied all his needs, including a more varied diet, and would always be there to support and guide him. No wonder this brought the quiet contentment he spoke about.

Our faithful Lord patiently waits

In a similar way, through all the changing scenes of life, our Lord will never leave or forsake us. It is our neglect of him that spoils the intended relationship, not his withdrawal from us. This negligence leaves us spiritually starved and emotionally vulnerable. Perversely, some will blame God for any hurt they feel—like the alienated child—refuse to be won over by a reminder of his unfailing love. Disconnected, they lack the understanding and patience that his Spirit would willingly provide in times of stress. But God never gives up hope that they will return to him and learn his loving ways: once the relationship with him has been established, only disobedience will cause the

[37] Psalm 131:2

Lord to hide his face. Even then his compassionate heart will long to take back the wanderer.[38]

We regularly need to remember that we have been told not to grumble.[39] To disobey this dishonours our Lord, because he cares about every detail of our lives – which means that we can have confidence in asking for grace when we are facing a trial which would otherwise be hard to endure. It is often the sudden irritations that provoke the loudest complaints, until we learn to keep in step with the Spirit and rely on his control. Cooperation with God is the way to find greater contentment.

For most of us the learning curve has not yet reached its apex, yet the lover of our souls gradually helps us to grow in the grace and knowledge of our Lord and Saviour Jesus Christ.[40] Of him it was said that people were amazed at the gracious words that came from his lips[41] – and wouldn't it be wonderful if such words came out of our lips, even under pressure? This could

---

[38] Isaiah 54:7-8
[39] 1 Corinthians 10:10
[40] 2 Peter 3:18
[41] Luke 4:22

so impress others that they ask us the reason for the grace that we are showing.

Notable examples of waiting on God

The Old Testament stories of Abraham, Joseph and Moses all tell of long years of waiting for God to fulfil his promises. Reading through them we find relatively few complaints, despite their respective trials of childlessness, unjust imprisonment and endless wandering in the wilderness. Their faith was greatly tested, but also strengthened as they trusted in God – and in time, he fulfilled his purposes for all of them. In the roll of honour of Hebrews 11, each is recorded as a man of outstanding faith.

Despite being a prominent religious leader, Paul had probably been a hasty, intolerant man before Jesus met him on the Damascus road and began his training as an apostle. This included God's allowing him to go through the severe sufferings we have already talked about, and many more.[42] Even so, Paul included these in the hardships through which he had learned to be content. We would do well to take note, even in our

---

[42] 2 Corinthians 11:23-30

smaller trials. God's purposes are always good, and in their fulfilment we too can find contentment.

4. Since you ask...

A friend of mine regularly attends a hospital clinic, but recently said that he no longer asks other patients how they are. An enquiry is always met with a long list of complaints, together with a blow-by-blow account of treatment they've endured and still anticipate. This remains the topic of general conversation but, although he has endured much more than anyone else in the room, he now chooses not to enter the discussion after realising that a new patient, caught up in the prevailing discontent, had become visibly uneasy as he foresaw an unexpectedly painful time ahead. As one bad apple in a basket contaminates the rest, so grumbling will adversely affect other people.

Who complains most?

Today I had a visit from two English missionaries on leave from South Africa, and I asked whether they find the same whinging there as the Australian I quoted in the Introduction found amongst the British. They didn't know where to start! The weather, the national economy, the political situation, deteriorating community spirit, a tendency to hark back to the good old days – they have found all these, and more, to be common complaints among the better-off South Africans, much as they find them here at home.

Their own work is with very poor and often very sick African orphans, who are cared for as one big happy family in a Christian community. In the communities where the children were born, alcoholism is rife, poorly-tended paraffin heaters start frequent fires, access to running water is a luxury, and healthcare is patchy, as are many amenities taken for granted in the developed world. The problems posed by the simple need to survive are many, but complaints of any kind are surprisingly few. Most people have time for each other and are ready to help when they can, and the regular grumbles of those who are better off stand in stark contrast to this kindlier norm in poorer communities. Of course, there will be exceptions in both groups, but my friends said that the differences between them are notable.

Carrying each other's burdens

The biblical mandate to carry each other's burdens adds that doing this fulfils the law of Christ[43] – and Jesus' greatest commandment links self-giving love for a neighbour with total devotion of the heart, soul and mind to God.[44] We need him to help us to understand how to offer whole-hearted care to each other, warmed by his love, instead of handing it out reluctantly as cold charity.

As low wage growth continues to be the norm for many in the Western world, so do complaints about it. But the psalmist David turned first to God with his grievances, giving us a good model by encouraging us to trust in God as a safe refuge at all times. To 'find rest' in him is to find contentment. Burdened hearts can confidently be poured out to him.[45] David knew that when pursuit of material wellbeing dominates, spiritual poverty follows. Jesus lived very simply and

---

[43] Galatians 6:2
[44] Matthew 22:34-40
[45] Psalm 62:5-8

warned that no-one can serve both God and money.[46] His own choice was to serve his Father God in humility, a lifestyle he calls us to follow.[47]

What's mine is *not* my own

Regardless of wealth, when we see tight-fistedness it's easy for us to see it as a sign of a mean spirit, but even some who think of themselves as generous have not realised that in fact their possessions possess them. It seems normal for people to want a desirable residence, stylish contemporary furniture, and an impressive car similar to those of their friends. After all, there is a certain standard to be kept up. Yet in other parts of the world, such luxuries are undreamed of.

A number of years ago I visited a family in Uganda. The widowed mother and her three children – two girls and a teenage boy – occupied one room in a ramshackle house that held several other poor families. The roof leaked, cows trampled mud up to the door, and their oven was a small basketful of charcoal outside the house. The room inside was furnished for

---

[46] Matthew 6:24
[47] Matthew 11:28-29

three, with one bed, two broken chairs, and pegs on the wall acting as a wardrobe. As we were leaving, the younger daughter took tight hold of my hand and said, 'Let me come with you.' Can you imagine that? She was later helped to train as a midwife by a young English friend.

How can we bridge such a gap? My lifestyle and the lifestyle of that family are poles apart. It is not enough to say, as someone once remarked to me, 'They have never known anything different', as if that excused me from taking any action at all. Yet the need in the world is so vast that many purses would have to be emptied in any effort to meet it all.

As ever, the Bible offers counsel. This time it expands on 'the grace of giving'.[48] The most important example is that of the Lord Jesus Christ who, though he was rich, became poor in order to enrich humanity with his goodness and mercy. Paul urged equality, as when asking wealthier followers of Christ to share with poorer ones. Having first given themselves to the Lord (including all that they own), those who can do so should give generously and cheerfully to help those in

---

[48] 2 Corinthians 8:7-9, 12

greater need – and to this, practical Paul adds that they should give what they have, not what they do not have. They should not risk becoming as destitute as their intended recipients.

Although Paul was speaking about money, gifts are not always of cash. Time, skills and prayer are all acceptably effective offerings – the last undergirding all the others. Peter includes hospitality among the offerings which are to be made without grumbling[49] – and indeed the Philippians are told by Paul to do *everything* 'without grumbling or arguing.'[50]

Appropriate giving must be decided individually and prayerfully, always remembering Jesus' example of loving self-sacrifice. For some this might involve paying school fees for children of a Christian family overseas instead of taking an annual holiday abroad. Some might prayerfully decide that they are able to do both, and should not be (enviously?) criticised for that. Our Lord wants his people to have proper rest and relaxation in order to serve him better.[51] Yet it has to be said that when he suggested to the tired disciples

---

[49] 1 Peter 4:9
[50] Philippians 2:14
[51] Matthew 11:28

that it was time to take a break, their holiday was just a trip across the lake to be greeted by a great crowd on the other side. After complaining that they would never find enough food for everyone, they were set to work serving over five thousand people with a miraculously-provided and satisfying picnic.[52]

God's generous gifts

In the book of 1 Chronicles, we read the story of David's preparations for building the temple in Jerusalem. At great expense David had amassed all the building materials that were needed for the splendid temple that his son, Solomon, would eventually build. His prayer of dedication acknowledged God as the source of wealth and honour, ending with a phrase to make our own: 'Everything comes from you, and we have given you only what comes from your hand.'[53]

The apostle Paul learned to live both in plenty and in want, and to be content with either.[54] In time, with David's prayer in mind, we could perhaps learn the same lesson.

[52] Mark 6:31-44
[53] 1 Chronicles 29:10-14
[54] Philippians 4:12

5. Nobody talks to me

Emperor Frederick II of Sicily is reputed to have conducted several heartless experiments on humans great and small during his reign in the 13th century. One of them involved a group of infants who were to be brought up with no personal interaction – no talking, smiling or anything other than the physical care needed to keep them alive. He had hoped that when they spoke at last it would be in Hebrew – but the experiment was never completed as they all died, starved of all tokens of love.

A baby of a few months old was once brought to see me, with the complaint that he was thought to be blind. As I examined him, I made the usual faces we make to interest babies and chatted to him. Wide-eyed, he made delighted responses. His mother exclaimed, 'But you are talking to him. I never talk to him.' Like Emperor Frederick she expected her son to start talking spontaneously, but – lesson learned – he would not share the fate of those young Sicilians. Parents greet their child's first words with great excitement even if less doting observers find them hard to understand. Love greatly helps interpretation.

Communication matters

When a country is hit by hurricanes, or has a power strike, one of the greatest inconveniences is getting messages through when lines of communication are down. Natives of the Kalahari Desert are said to have a certain beating in the chest to tell them of important news. The proverbial tom-tom drums served the same purpose in West Africa, much like smoke signals elsewhere in the world. More important than these is regular interpersonal communication between people without any intervening screens. Communication is so important for nourishing relationships.

The wife of a surgeon once came to see me, complaining that her husband never talked to her. She meant that he had no small talk – his conversation, like his work, was incisive and to the point. One of the tasks of marriage guidance counsellors is to help to open up communication between partners. Without it the partnership can struggle to survive.

The same applies to friendship. One of the fears of shy young children starting school is that nobody will want to talk to them or play with them. Such complaints are usually unfounded – chatterboxes are everywhere, start young and survive for years. Even so, careful attention to playground conversations will often reveal that each child is talking about a different subject. What matters more than the content of their exchange is the contact with someone else. This applies to many adults too, throughout our lives. Lonely old people have been known to phone for an ambulance simply to have someone else to talk to. Stroke victims whose speech is affected can make valiant but frustrated efforts to converse, which are equally frustrating for those trying to respond. The same applies to people who are born deaf, and who remain mute unless they are selflessly taught and helped by someone who is well-versed in sign language. While hard work this is so much better than to give in to the impulse to steer clear, complaining about the difficulties of communication.

Sometimes people who venture into a strange church complain afterwards that no-one spoke to them. I once tried this out when attending a big city church overseas. Instead of scurrying to the door as I might otherwise have done, I stood my ground to see what would happen. Eventually my hopes were raised when the vicar's wife spotted me and approached – but only to tell me, 'Coffee is through there', pointing to a side room. I fared no better there, lingering hopefully and clutching my cup of coffee. I saw folk busily engaged with their friends, but I didn't have the temerity to interrupt them – and neither did they notice the solitary stranger in their midst. Admittedly this was an unusual (though memorable) experience for me, either at home or overseas, but it taught me to look out for people who are looking a bit lost after a service and to go for a chat with them. Happily my present church family has a team who welcome people as they come in, and after the service make sure that no visitor complains that this is such an unfriendly church that they'll not come back again.

Last words

There have been some terrible tragedies in Britain during the last two decades, as well as the suicide bombings on 9/11 in the USA. In many emergencies, people have been trapped and unable to escape, and the last messages from their mobile phones have become exceedingly precious to their families. These messages are almost always words of love rather than complaint.

The Bible gives us examples of significant last words. Isaiah foretells Jesus' lack of complaint before those who would condemn him to death; 'He was oppressed and afflicted, yet he did not open his mouth.'[55] This prophecy was fulfilled when, after his arrest, Jesus was brought before the Sanhedrin. He stayed silent in the face of his accusers, so much so that the chief of them, the high priest, was the one to complain, 'Are you not going to answer?'[56] But Jesus remained silent, and gave no answer. When he was asked directly, 'Are you the Messiah?' his 'I am' brought the charge of blasphemy and ultimately the death sentence. Even as he was crucified, Jesus' cry was for his executioners to be forgiven.[57] Complaint was not in his nature, even when he was so sorely pressed.

---

[55] Isaiah 53:7
[56] Mark 14:60-64
[57] Luke 23:34

After Jesus' resurrection, as he was about to leave his disciples, his last recorded words to them promised them the power of his Spirit as they became his witnesses.[58] This would prove to be a costly commission – we have details of words spoken by Stephen, the first Christian martyr, as he was stoned to death. He, too, did not complain, but prayed forgiveness for those who were murdering him.[59]

Sharing the best news of all

Around us, every day, there are likely to be people who are discontented with their circumstances. Some will live alone and can be very lonely, perhaps with only a pet to talk to. We need to be alert to clues they may drop, and be ready to offer a friendly greeting. Sometimes this opens up a conversation during which we can receive the fulfilment of Jesus' promise that his Spirit will give us words to say in difficult circumstances.[60] We can rely on his inspiration when we're trying to help lonely souls to find a faithful friend in him. It may be a meaningful phrase that we unintentionally use which starts someone on a

---

[58] Acts 1:8
[59] Acts 7:52-60
[60] Mark 13:11

spiritual search, or we might simply be a link in the human chain that will finally draw them to Jesus. His written word will provide messages of comfort, and his people will offer companionship – but somebody needs to have seized the opportunity to break the silence and so initiate such a possible sequence.

Jesus drew close to lonely people,[61] and brought healing to social outcasts.[62] Whatever we do in his name for any such people, we do for him, and he is well pleased by it.[63] This could be so simple an act as visiting an old person who is unable to get out, or giving a little food to a beggar instead of offering money that might go on drugs. I recently heard of a young mother who regularly took her little girl to give a pack of sandwiches to a man living on the street and have a chat with him. He greeted them with obvious pleasure and affection, knowing their names and receiving their gift of love with gratitude. Acting in the Lord's name it had seemed the most natural thing to do. Follow that!

---

[61] Luke 7:11-15
[62] Mark 5:1-20; Luke 17:12-19
[63] Matthew 25:31-40

After telling a very similar story, Jesus said, 'Go and do likewise.'[64] There are countless opportunities waiting for us to act in the same generous spirit.

---

[64] Luke 10:37

6. Is anybody there?

Some people complain about not having anyone to complain to. Many of us will have had this kind of experience on the telephone, when we're looking for a straight answer to a straight question from a business or an organisation, only to be told to press sequential buttons to receive a choice of information which we don't need, until the last option tells us to wait for assistance. At last we hear a human voice – but the relief gives way to more frustration if the voice goes on to tell us what number we are in the queue.

The temptation is to complain to the speaker about our wasted time, but of course the protest would only be to a recording. It can be even worse if we go online in our search. Complaints about computers are common – they are such useful tools most of the time, but become another source of frustration when we can't find the exact words for the piece of information we need (or the font suddenly changes size and colour, as mine has just done).

Adverse comments on the weather probably top the list of complaints which are to be heard in the UK, and it is no good shouting about an unwelcome forecast to the television screen. It was accordingly a great pleasure for me today when a shop assistant ran through the wonderful variety of conditions that we have in Britain: sunshine and showers, thunder and lightning, frost and snow, the changes to be expected as our four seasons come and go, as well as some that are unexpected. As he warmed to his theme, he explained that, in his view, all this makes a very favourable contrast to the constant blazing sunshine experienced in some other countries. He had pointed this out to his eleven-year-old son when they were flying over a country in the throes of drought. The grass was brown and parched, in contrast to the green and pleasant land they would see as they came in to land at home. To find someone who actually appreciates our weather, and was teaching his son to do so, made such a welcome change. The Lord is good to us and we should not complain so much when it rains.

Hearing voices and reading messages

Like all technological advances, computers can be used for good or ill, and cause complaints when machines are misused (by others, of course). Smartphones can provide us with all kinds of useful information, but they also offer access to paedophiles and pornography. Their use can become addictive, completely occupying the user's attention regardless of their present company. Some parents ban telephones from the meal table, but we can go to any restaurant and see diners with phones out on the table. Texting even goes on during church services – and not for note-taking about the sermon. Something which was originally designed to improve communication can actually push out potentially more rewarding personal input, while inattention to the rest of the world holds other dangers. With his phone glued to his ear a pedestrian was once about to walk into the path of my moving car until he noticed it at the last minute.

Some hard-pressed doctors tend to concentrate on their computer screen for reports, information and laboratory results without having much eye contact with their patients. To reduce hospital waiting lists, some follow-up appointments are now being conducted by phone, meaning doctors miss non-verbal cues that would allow them to make a clearer assessment of their patient's wellbeing – and of course, in time this could become another cause for complaint.

Complaints that don't get through

In other parts of the world many cries go unheard. A recent report told of very young Indian girls being used as slave labour. Like the ancient Israelites, they are forced to make bricks under harsh conditions and for a mere pittance, where factory managers will beat them if they fail to fulfil their allotted quota. Others, of an age when they should be at school, work from dawn to dusk creating fine embroidery, and their beautiful handiwork goes overseas to be eagerly purchased by people who would be horrified to learn about the original conditions under which the work was done.

Back on home territory, there are many others whose cries are muted. Not long ago I was in a shop, impatiently waiting my turn, long after the previous transaction had been completed, as the assistant and customer stood still chatting. I was about to indicate my irritation, but decided that a better course was to join in the conversation, which was becoming increasingly negative. Chief targets for complaint were our National Health Service, the government, and the international situation. I put in a word for the health service and for the rest commented on the Lord's complete control.

As the previous customer and I were leaving the shop together, she said that not many people mentioned the Lord these days. She went with me to my car and a moment or two later astonished me by bursting into tears. Between sobs she told me that if she had not come to the shop that morning, she had planned to kill herself. No wonder the conversation at the counter had been spiralling downwards. I suggested that we should pray, took her hands through the car window and asked the Lord Jesus to give his peace to her troubled mind. She calmed somewhat after indicating that she was under medical supervision, and departed. I made myself available if she should wish to see me again, and later I left a note for her at the shop and asked others to pray with me for her. I was so relieved to hear that, weeks later, she had picked up the note. There has been no more direct contact since then, but

I know that the Lord who so clearly timed that meeting will keep her in his care.

Depression often wears a mask, and there must be many who are hiding their struggle. The Holy Spirit is well able to arrange for them to meet someone who might unconsciously say something helpful that could contribute to their eventual healing.

Discontent breeds complaint

Bank clerks and post office workers have long worked behind protective screens, and other agencies have recently followed suit, lest the complaints of the people in the waiting queue become threatening. The strongest screen I have ever seen was at a bar in central Australia which had become a tourist exhibit. The customers often became drunk and violent, and the bartender's fortification clearly indicated anticipation of bitter complaints from an aggrieved public.

In the major cities of the world, complaints abound about increasingly rude and anti-social behaviour, of gang warfare and of stabbings frequent enough for the scared local populace to seek safety indoors. Such violence is often fuelled by alcohol or drug abuse.

Offenders complain about a variety of circumstances which, added together, mean that they feel unloved. All too often, their upbringing has been short of people who are consistently there for them, and for many, arousing hostile attention seems better than having no attention at all.

Here is another gap which public-spirited Christians are trying to bridge by expressing the long-suffering love of God. The Christian mother of a boy who was involved with a gang courageously invited him and his mates to come home for a hot meal, which was the first home-cooked food most of them had eaten for a long time. Her love touched them and encouraged them to stop being a menace to the neighbourhood. One of the lads commented what a difference it had made to feel that somebody cared about them.

An ever-attentive ear

Jesus told stories about those who for a time deliberately refused to hear the pleas of someone in need, because it was inconvenient,[65] or simply out of hardness of heart.[66] In contrast, he told how his Father

---

[65] Luke 11:5-8
[66] Luke 18:1-5

always answers those who call on him. He hears and answers the cry of those who 'cry unto him day and night.'[67] Some may be questioning his existence as they ask, 'Is anybody there?' – but he is always there, and may reveal himself first through the love of one his dedicated followers. The psalmist David said that the Lord's ears are attentive to the cry of the righteous,[68] except when sin is cherished in their hearts.[69] For all of us, confession will bring forgiveness and a clean sheet,[70] with the assurance that God's love endures forever.[71]

What a lot we have to be thankful for – and we have someone to thank as well. There is always somebody there to help us,[72] so we are never left frustrated when we call out to him. He does not deal in automatic messages, and his written word will always have something to say that is pertinent to our need.

Is anybody there? Yes, always.

---

[67] Luke 18:7
[68] Psalm 34:15
[69] Psalm 66:18
[70] 1 John 1:9
[71] Psalm 136
[72] Hebrews 7:25

7. I'm so scared

After six years of intensive study, a group of nervous medical students came together to hear the results of their final examinations. If they passed, they would soon be licensed to practise as doctors; if they failed, it would mean more study, and repeated exams.

The atmosphere was tense as the Dean of the Medical School read out the names of the candidates. As one of the men heard that he had passed, he fainted. He had been so afraid of failure that the relief literally felled him.

The feeling of fear can range from apprehension to panic, depending on the size of the threat and the personality and life experience of the threatened.

Small children may be scared of the dark, but with maturity they will realise that twinkling stars and moonshine can only be properly appreciated in the dark. The more spiritually-minded, and those who are old enough to grasp the significance of parables and metaphors, can see that even the dark night of the soul can hold gleams of light, which often reach us through the love of others.

Apprehension

Most of us will have experienced apprehension at one time or another, for a variety of reasons. A visit to the dentist or doctor can make us worry about the consultation itself, as well as about what might follow. For many, impending surgery and its implications can move apprehension up a notch into real anxiety, especially if the diagnosis is life-changing, or even life-threatening.

The young doctor-to-be mentioned at the beginning of this chapter would probably be already apprehensive when he was called to interview for a hospital post, and even more so on his first day at work. What if he made a mistake in diagnosis or treatment and someone sued him for malpractice? An apprehensive mindset comes with a never-ending list of 'what ifs.' When one of them is realised a state of alarm follows.

Alarm

During World War 2, sirens warned apprehensive people in cities of the approach of enemy bombers, and told them that they needed to take cover. A fire alarm alerts the householder of danger. The wail of a passing ambulance with its flashing lights warns drivers and pedestrians to make way. In an intensive care unit, unusual bleeping of a ventilator calls for urgent attention. Alarms which raise apprehension should galvanise us to immediate action, otherwise anxiety grows.

It can be dangerous to ignore or complain about alarms, as certain world leaders have discovered after first denying the reality of global warming and later of the Covid-19 pandemic. Alarms can have good effects when they are heeded and bad effects when they are ignored, as many of us have found out when we had drowsily switched off a ringing alarm clock, only to be made late for work.

Anxiety

Whereas some people are born worriers, and will find a way to fret in any circumstances, others have genuinely serious anxieties. Will they be able to pay the mortgage, or get healthcare for their children? A growing number across the world worry about where the next meal will come from, especially if that meal depends on a good harvest from their own small patch of land without access to the food banks which are available in better-off societies. Starvation looms.

In such poor countries, sickness or serious illness are huge causes for concern, and for some, getting to a medical centre in the first place would break the bank. In Britain we are so blessed to have a National Health Service that was set up to be freely available to everyone at the point of need; yet letters of complaint regularly arrive on administrative desks across the NHS.

Terror

In countries with Christian minorities, there is often good reason for believers to be fearful. Even innocent activities like going to the well for water can meet fierce opposition from neighbours who oppose the presence of Christians in their community. Children from Christian families run the gauntlet of animosity every day on their way to school, and on arrival can be cold-shouldered by teachers and classmates alike. In some countries Christian women are persecuted both for being Christian and for being women. Fanatics who are intent on destroying anyone of a different faith can breed terror in their intended victims, who flee if they are able.

In 2019, representatives of extremist Islam in northern Nigeria killed 2,983 Christians, including whole communities of believers. Failure to attend the mosque with the majority can result in severe beatings, even for young Christians. Pastors disappear, their tortured dead bodies abandoned and found later by their grieving families. Exhibitions of skulls in Rwandan and Turkish churches put into perspective the anti-Christian attitude which some believers in parts of the so-called developed world complain of in their own settings. Persecution comes in many forms, some more painful than others – yet members of the suffering church refuse to give up their loyalty to Jesus, in whom they have found a love and liberty unknown to their persecutors. Such believers are encouraging examples to those of us whose suffering is so much less.

Panic

As I write, the Covid-19 viral pandemic of 2020 is killing thousands of people worldwide, and many people are living in a state of acute anxiety. Panic-buying by those who are able to stockpile has left supermarket shelves denuded, while people with less purchasing power go without. A hungry nurse wept when going off-duty after a long day working with infected patients because she could find nothing left to buy for her supper. A normally obliging mechanic at our local garage would usually have come to collect my car when it needed attention, but during the pandemic he refused. He had panic in his voice as he said to me, 'I'm not coming out. I have a young family to think of.' The fact that my car would not contaminate him carried no weight – he was clearly panicking about meeting a possible carrier somewhere between his garage and mine. The garage was closed soon afterwards.

On the positive side, hundreds of thousands of volunteers responded to the call to help the hard-pressed NHS, despite many admitting to feeling very scared. Some would drive ambulances, or deliver medical supplies to hospital, or take food to people unable to safely leave their homes. Thousands of the volunteers were health professionals and senior medical students. A number of people who were working on the front line were seriously unnerved by the daily loss of life they were witnessing, while none of their patients were allowed visits from loved ones – even when they were dying. Some health professionals lost their own lives to the virus, and this gave rise to complaints about inadequate supplies of protective clothing for them and for staff in care homes. Bus and taxi drivers also complained, being threatened by their proximity to passengers who might be carrying the virus. People of colour were especially at risk. Domestic violence increased.

There was a general reduction in traffic, as people conformed to government rules on restricted travel. Pedestrians from different homes kept the statutory two metres apart on the one daily outing they were allowed. In a society that had felt so dominated by self-interest, such widespread and considerate thought for others was as uplifting as seeing bright stars in a dark sky.

Among all the circumstances outlined in this chapter (and more) some people will have complained about their misfortune. How may they be brought closer to acceptance, let alone contentment – or at least to being less scared?

Help for the fearful

First, even when the conversation can't be face to face but by phone, helpers should take the complaints seriously and empathise with the situation. The opportunity to unload can itself be therapeutic when somebody cares enough to listen.

There are practical ways to offer encouragement to the socially isolated, such as doing shopping for them, posting letters or leaving a posy of flowers or a casserole on the doorstep. Spending time making protective clothing for health workers would improve social isolation and possibly save lives.

Assurance of prayer may be the only thing we are able to offer those being frightened, whether at home or abroad. In the UK we can also advocate for issues around persecution to be raised in Parliament, or give financial support to organisations like Open Doors who work to help the suffering church overseas (01993 4610015). Closer to home, we can give support to organisations who work to help people in debt, such as Church Action on Poverty (info@church-poverty.org.uk)

Offering hope is so important. This pandemic will pass, and in *all* circumstances the best hope on offer is found in the Bible:

> Proverbs 3:5-6 – Trust in the Lord with all your heart...; in all your ways submit to him and he will make your paths straight.
>
> Psalm 56:3-4 – When I am afraid, I put my trust in you. In God...I trust and am not afraid. What can mere mortals do to me?
>
> Psalm 46:1 – God is our refuge and strength, an ever-present help in trouble.

God has his own purposes when he permits our difficulties, one of which could be to strengthen our faith. We slowly learn to hold on to the promise he has made to us, to be with us always.[73] We need not panic when we have such an omnipotent companion, for '...in

---

[73] Matthew 28:20

all things God works for the good of those who love him, who have been called according to his purpose'.[74]

This is our hope

I am writing this at Easter time, when many of us will be thinking about the love of God as it is expressed through Jesus, who paid the penalty for our sins on the cross and opened access to the Father for us. The resurrection that followed, energised by the Holy Spirit, gives us hope that death itself has been conquered. Many people have feared death all their lives, but for those who love God death will be an entrance into the home he has prepared for us, not simply an exit from earthly life.[75]

Even those who don't share such faith can see that some good things have come out of the terrible pandemic of Covid-19. A greater spirit of togetherness has emerged between people, in spite of enforced physical separation. It is as though we are being refined – never a comfortable process – but it is to be hoped that a more generous spirit will prevail, despite forebodings of coming economic hardship. The

---

[74] Romans 8:28
[75] John 14:2

preciousness of personal relationships is enhanced when they are threatened by sickness and separation. We can hope that this new awareness will last beyond the pandemic that is posing the threat.

Whatever it is that makes us fearful, those who hope in the Lord will renew their strength.[76] Anchored in his perfect love, fear is driven out.[77] With that assurance, we have good reason not to feel so scared.

---

[76] Isaiah 40:31
[77] 1 John 4:18

8. Surely church people don't complain?

If we had never been in a church, we might fondly imagine that a church family would be completely harmonious, its members united in loyalty to the Lord, even if they are not uniform in their ways of showing it. This, indeed, is what Jesus intended[78] – but sadly it is not always the case. Disunity emerges when members disagree, often over petty matters rather than grave doctrinal issues. Complaints crop up about the times and styles of services, the length and content of sermons, the position of various pieces of church furniture, who has been chosen "in preference to me" for a particular group or position in the church's

---

[78] John 17:11

organisation and, a frequent source of complaint, the style of music and choice of hymns.

I don't understand half of it

The Jews of Jesus' day thought of themselves as God's chosen people, yet when he spoke truth to them in parables, they did not understand him. When he claimed to be the bread of life, for example, they debated what he could possibly mean.[79] Similarly, in the Book of Acts, in chapter 7 we read how the first martyr, Stephen, had the same problem with his accusers. Although they all knew the Old Testament scriptures well, Stephen, 'full of the Holy Spirit', recognised that many of the ancient prophecies foretold the life, sufferings and resurrection of Jesus, whereas his opponents 'always' resisted the Holy Spirit. That is why they had killed their Messiah, and why they would stone Stephen to death. It follows that we must be open to the Holy Spirit of God and Christ[80] as we read our Bibles. They are not merely human words but God's, and through them his Spirit longs to shape our thoughts and attitudes.[81]

---

[79] John 6:35-52
[80] Romans 8:9
[81] 1 Thessalonians 2:13; Ephesians 6:17; Hebrews 4:12-13

Just as the earthly Jesus rebuked complaining then, perhaps he would do the same today when religious people fail to seek the help of his Holy Spirit as they try to apply God's word. By preferring instead to indulge in what they like to call 'higher' criticism, many people miss out badly, making a show of merely formal religion, or intellectual wordplay, without encountering God's promised truth.[82] Critics like this can come from all walks of life. One young woman complained, 'I didn't know what they were talking about,' after she had followed a Bible study course that was designed to enlighten. Her attendance had perhaps been more as a curious spectator than a genuine seeker after truth.

I don't like the music

The popular usage of the phrase 'the worship' to mean the sung part of a service misses the deeper meaning of the word. Our spiritual act of worship, as defined by Paul, is 'to offer your bodies as a living sacrifice'.[83] Elsewhere in the scriptures, congregational singing is referred to as 'making music to the Lord', or speaking to one another 'with psalms, hymns and songs from

---

[82] John 14:26
[83] Romans 12:1

the Spirit' when music is 'made from your heart to the Lord'.[84] Fervent songs of genuine praise can inspire truly sacrificial worship, and I would not want my concern about the deeper meaning of the word to become divisive – but the risk is that in 'having a good sing', the singers go into automatic. For example, I have heard the third verse of the hymn 'When I survey the wondrous cross', which describes the awesome suffering of our Lord Jesus, belted out with the same enthusiasm as the rest of the hymn, that in any case, was composed to assist contemplation.

Old Testament references to praise and worship include descriptions of both in the books written by Ezra and Nehemiah. They recorded the celebrations associated with the rebuilding of Jerusalem and its temple, including a reminder of God's law, given through Moses and so often broken. As Ezra opened the book of the law to read it aloud, the people all stood up. Nehemiah reports, 'Ezra praised the Lord, the great God; and all the people lifted up their hands and responded, "Amen! Amen!" Then they bowed

---

[84] Psalm 27:6; Psalm 98:5; Ephesians 5:19

down and worshipped the Lord with their faces to the ground.'[85]

In the stories of Jesus' birth, the Magi 'bowed down and worshipped him'[86] as they offered their treasures, while the shepherds returned to their flocks 'glorifying and praising God.'[87] The women who were first to meet the resurrected Jesus 'clasped his feet and worshipped him.'[88]

Perhaps I am being a little pedantic in making this distinction between praise and worship, but we should never forget Paul's definition of worship as a costly act, even as we offer up our voices.

Some persecuted believers in the suffering church overseas are offering up life itself; but they can sometimes be heard singing as they face their execution.

[85] Nehemiah 8:5-6
[86] Matthew 2:11
[87] Luke 2:20
[88] Matthew 28:9

Havens of peace and concord?

Sadly, the expectation of harmony is not always fulfilled in some churches. I am blessed by being part of a loving and gifted church family, who are enthusiastic to share the love of Jesus with our local community. At a church in a different area from ours, during a gap between one vicar's retirement and the appointment of their successor, three powerful women took over the leadership and refused to relinquish control when the new man came. They so undermined his ministry with their complaints and criticisms that he lost heart and resigned. Unity is also spoiled when self-appointed leaders of different cliques vie with each other for greater influence. Elsewhere, even our gifts can become reasons for conflict – as when someone of an independent mindset complains about someone else whose gift for organisation can be interpreted as officiousness.

Of course, money can be a reason for discord as well. A church may disagree about how much of their income should go to international aid organisations, with some members complaining that the new boiler should take priority instead. Appeals for support for the local food bank or night shelter, or for overseas missionaries, may find no response, with the complaint that the church 'always wants more of your money'. Stinginess limits generosity, and is comparable to the scrupulous tithing practised by wealthy Pharisees in Jesus' day. They would even painstakingly tithe their garden herbs, but would do so without any genuine care for the poor. A veneer that suggested godliness hid attitudes which were far from holy. Such actions are foreign to our Lord's teaching, despite the fact that they are happening in the context of the Christian church.

Beyond the local church, historic differences and mutual dislike can flare up into actual conflict, as in Northern Ireland. At one time it was dangerous for Protestants and Roman Catholics to venture into a residential area mainly occupied by the other party. There, loyalty to Christ gave way to what was effectively tribalism. In many other places church can be a kind of social club, sometimes resounding with criticism and complaint. Observing this, unbelievers can see selfishness and disharmony as the normal outworking of Christianity, and cry 'Hypocrisy!' before turning elsewhere for a more inviting religion.

Such things ought not to be. In fact, we in the church are the body of Christ, under his headship and sharing his generous love. The true church worldwide is made up of brothers and sisters of the Lord Jesus, all members of the same family.[89]

Sharing the love of Jesus

In contrast to all this division, a visitor to a vibrant and generous church once complained, 'You talk too much about Jesus.' She did not understand that what she saw and heard was an illustration of cause and effect. The church's exuberance was a heartfelt response to our Lord's sacrificial love.

In any case, a *Christ*ian church, as a body of believers, should be proclaiming *Christ* and demonstrating his love through the pouring out of their own, first back to him and then out to others. As the first fruit of the Holy Spirit, self-giving and mutual love would also help us to resolve differences which are being expressed within the church family before they cause serious schism. That should be our prayer.

I once heard of two senior church members who were at odds with each other. They both attended a large Christian convention, but one of them turned up late

---

[89] John 1:12-13

for a crowded teaching session. He could only find one vacant seat – next to his rival! The coincidence, along with the message they heard that day, convicted them both of their wrong attitude, and they begged each other's forgiveness. They left the meeting together, their broken relationship restored.

Like lubrication for a complex piece of machinery, the patient development of mutual love can gently ease away our complaints and divisions. Jesus instructed his disciples shortly before his crucifixion: 'Love one another as I have loved you.'[90]

Easier said than done? Inspiration may come from quietly and prayerfully reading that favourite hymn:

> *When I survey the wondrous cross*
> *On which the Prince of glory died,*
> *My richest gain I count but loss,*
> *And pour contempt on all my pride.*
>
> *Forbid it, Lord, that I should boast,*
> *Save in the death of Christ my God:*
> *All the vain things that charm me most*

---

[90] John 15:12

I sacrifice them to His blood.

See from His head, His hands, His feet,
Sorrow and love flow mingled down:
Did e'er such love and sorrow meet,
Or thorns compose so rich a crown?

Were the whole realm of nature mine,
That were an offering far too small,
Love so amazing, so divine,
Demands my soul, my life, my all.

With due respect to that hymn's author, Isaac Watts, we may choose to say instead that God, who is love, *'shall have'* my soul, my life my all – and that will include my relationships with others. To be united with each other and with our Lord is to be well on the way to contentment.

9. Sweet contentment despite the trials

When my brother was 93 years old, his lovely and gifted wife died. He missed her hugely, but instead of complaining, he expressed gratitude for the many happy years of their marriage. With limited mobility, he was cared for at home by a resident carer, a thoughtful young man from Zimbabwe named Kudzai, who said that he never heard George complain. Old friends came regularly to make chamber music together, and George skilfully played his recorder, still with evident enjoyment. I once asked him how he was feeling, and was touched when he replied, 'I'm quite content really.' George died as he had lived, quietly and peacefully, just short of his 94th birthday.

Content whatever the circumstances

Paul, however, led a very different life. Earlier, in chapter 3 of this book, we read about the many ways in which he suffered. He listed most of them twice in the second letter to the Corinthians,[91] indicating that they had marked him for life – and that Paul believed his readers needed to know that following Jesus would involve self-denial, and the taking up of a cross, just as Jesus had warned.[92] His catalogues of hardship were not presented as complaints but as a commentary which affirmed his apostolic authenticity and sacrificial lifestyle.

Unlike Paul, we are likely to complain when trials come our way. We need to find out how he wrested contentment from his adversity, as we have already seen from Philippians 4:12, and how we may do the same from ours. We will focus mainly on examples from his second list of sufferings in 2 Corinthians 11, although there is a lot of overlap with the first.

---

[91] 2 Corinthians 6:4-10; 2 Corinthians 11:23b-33
[92] Mark 8:34

Bombardment

The first record we have of Paul's physical persecution is in Acts 14.[93] After he and Barnabas had been taken for gods in Lystra (something they strenuously denied), they were pursued by Jews who were offended by their teaching. These men stirred up the previously adoring crowd to murderous mood. Paul was stoned, dragged out of the city and left for dead. The disciples who were with him gathered round, no doubt with fervent prayer. How relieved they must have been when he came round and got up. After an unspecified interval of teaching elsewhere, he bravely returned to the same city from which he had been dragged unconscious.

This episode demonstrates Paul's courage, but also how he had a clear calling – he was 'compelled to preach'.[94] The harsh experience in Lystra was possibly the catalyst that brought a young disciple from that city into his life. Years later he would refer to him as 'Timothy, my true son in the faith'.[95] God often brings

---

[93] Acts 14:8-20
[94] 1 Corinthians 9:16
[95] Acts 16:1; 1 Timothy 1:2

something good out of something bad, but we may often have to wait to recognise what that is.

All followers of Jesus are called to be his witnesses,[96] though not all are called to preach like Paul. Yet all those who belong to Christ are called to 'hold firmly' to confidence and hope.[97]

Members of the persecuted church overseas often need, and show, remarkable courage in the face of opposition such as Paul endured, yet they still keep their hope and faith in Christ Jesus. Those of us who do not know such flagrant hostility should not feel complacent. Instead we need to keep alert, protected by the spiritual armour we have been given,[98] and prepared for the devil's subtler attempts to knock us off course.

Our minds can be bombarded with unkind remarks and ungodly ideas, in the same way as Paul was pounded into unconsciousness with stones. Like him,

---

[96] Acts 1:8
[97] Hebrews 3:6
[98] Ephesians 6:10-18

we need to keep true to God's word, surrounded by prayerful friends and inspired by his Holy Spirit.

Endurance

Paul's sufferings must have included exhaustion from his journeys over difficult terrain, constantly on the move and often walking for miles, getting hungry, thirsty and cold, as well as being in danger from bandits. Overseas missionaries sometimes endure similar trials today. Perhaps Paul's most memorable flogging and imprisonment was in Philippi, as recorded in Acts 16, but his list of adversities suggests that this was far from the only time he had suffered like this. John Pollock, in his biography *Paul the Apostle* (1969), speculates that some of the lashings and beatings with rods mentioned in that list took place when the newly-converted Saul had been sent back home to Tarsus (for his safety!)[99] We read in Acts 9 that the Jews in Damascus and Jerusalem had already planned to kill him for his conversion, prompting his return to Tarsus. Pollock argues that Paul would not then have escaped the wrath and brutal vengeance of those loyal to the Tarsus synagogue.

---

[99] Acts 9:22-30

Similarly, members of the suffering church today often endure physical ill-treatment at the hands of those whose faith they have abandoned to follow Jesus. Three Christian women in Cameroon recently had an ear sliced off by extremists opposed to their faith. Members of the underground church can also be in danger from treacherous 'false brothers' like Paul's, who betray them when they have been driven to worshipping in secret. We should be thankful for our freedom to witness openly without such threats, although hostility can be expressed in other ways.

Shipwreck

In Acts 27 we find a riveting account of a great shipwreck, one of three experienced by Paul. This one happened when he was a prisoner under guard and it threatened all who sailed with him. At the height of the storm, Paul urged his frightened fellow passengers to take courage, saying that he had received a special message from the Lord that they would all be saved, though their ship would be broken into pieces. So it was – though Paul could not resist reminding them that the disaster would have been avoided if they had taken his advice in the first place and delayed the journey.

Much later, when writing to Timothy, Paul spoke of those who had 'shipwrecked their faith', losing the fight against the enemy of their souls and rejecting their belief in Jesus, ignoring pangs of conscience as they blasphemed against him.[100] Just as Paul had warned about the dangers of the voyage, so young believers should be taught that embarking on the new life in Christ is no guarantee that all will be plain sailing. 'Come to Jesus and everything will be all right' is a false message. Some do not survive the opposition that often threatens their new-found joy, and so risk their faith being shipwrecked unless they have been taught to expect these storms. Young faith needs to be carefully and lovingly nourished in the word of God, and introduced to the sustaining fellowship of fellow believers and the Holy Spirit. This needs watchful oversight, teaching and encouragement by seasoned believers who are willing to act as mentors, just as Paul urged his shipmates to 'keep up your courage' when they were together in stormy waters. This is still a strengthening message to share with any who struggle with temptations or hardships, and who would find it very natural to complain.

---

[100] 1 Timothy 1:18-20

As if the catalogue of his sufferings were not enough so far, Paul adds that he felt daily the pressure of his concern for all of the young churches. He had helped to start them – but had they continued in the faith? This was such a huge concern for Paul that it deserves another chapter.

10. God's purposes are always good

Occasionally ill-informed people will ask what local pastors do on weekdays, as Sunday seems to be the only day they work. It would probably be enlightening for them to present the question to one of those pastors in person and take note of the reaction. Taking good care of their flock is a demanding, time consuming task for church ministers – just ask their partners at home.

The young Corinthian church was one of the many which concerned Paul. Corinth was a major trading city in Greece, with all the temptations and immorality which are prevalent in big cities and ports everywhere. Idol worship was the chief religious practice of the city, with the temple of Aphrodite, goddess of love, being notorious as a centre of religious prostitution. There was a synagogue in the city as well, and there had therefore been a mixed reception to Paul's proclamation of the good news of Jesus' birth, life, sacrificial death, resurrection and ascension, and the promise of eternal life to those who believe in him. Despite opposition, a young church had been established in the city, whose members met in peoples' homes or in secluded places outside the city, as the threatened underground church often has to do today.

For some Corinthian church members, the moral laxity of the city's culture persisted, and they were rebuked by Paul in his first letter to them. He also dealt with some of their questions. The members of the Corinthian church needed to learn about the lifestyle and behaviour proper for Christians, so that they would 'shine like stars in the sky' in a 'warped and crooked culture', as Paul also exhorted the Philippians to do.[101] Both young and old still need to be reminded today, as the Corinthian church perhaps did then, that the all-too-prevalent habit of using the name of the

---

[101] Philippians 2:14-15

Lord God lightly, as an exclamation, is a form of blasphemy.[102]

Finding contentment

The same problems which concerned Paul still surface in young (and older) churches today, both overseas and at home. As we saw in chapter 8 of this book, church members are not immune from complaints and disharmony. Yet the great apostle said he had learned to find contentment. What can we learn from him about how to leave complaints behind, and be satisfied? There are a few different things that can help.

Like-minded Christian friends normally accompanied Paul throughout his travels, sometimes sharing his beatings. He and Silas encouraged each other, even in song, as they endured their painful imprisonment in Philippi. Disciples gathered round Paul when he had been stoned almost to death. Brothers and sisters in Christ should not neglect meeting together. It is vital that members of the church support each other, especially when individuals are finding church attendance difficult. Finding a prayer partner, or

---

[102] Exodus 20:7

joining a home Bible study group, both offer opportunities to share problems in confidence and recover perspective when we are hard-pressed. Mature believers should be watchful for any stragglers or strugglers, keep on praying for them, and quietly come to their aid when we can.

The word of God was constantly on Paul's lips, and the Holy Spirit inspired him to write the letters which now form a significant part of the New Testament. Occasionally, as during the shipwreck we read about in Acts 27, God gave him a special message of encouragement. We have to be careful of claims that 'the Lord said' something to someone unless what they report is backed by Scripture. There, we will find words of encouragement and guidance which the Holy Spirit will bring home to us in a special way when we need to hear them. If we are to experience this, we should not neglect our daily reading. Even a few verses, when we are stressed, may give us the message we need for that day. It is rare to hear an audible heavenly voice, as perhaps Paul did, but the Spirit may put ideas into our minds which are distinguishable from Satan's by always being in step with God's word. Sometimes it will be a relevant direct quote which impresses itself on the mind when we most need to hear it.

Years ago, I was working in the North of England, and I was called to an interview in London. When I went to catch the train on the morning of the interview, no train arrived. Timing was crucial for me to keep the appointment, and I began to worry. Then I noticed a framed poster on the platform quoting the verse, 'My times are in your hands'![103] I committed my deadline to those hands, waited for the next train, finally reached London some hours later, and ran for a taxi – which promptly broke down. In the end it was such a relief for me to get to the interview at all that it went very well. I was appointed to a lovely job at the seaside, which became an important rung on the ladder of my training as a paediatrician.

Prayerfulness is another important habit for keeping us focused on God. In his letters, Paul repeatedly urges his readers to pray, particularly throughout his letter to the Ephesians. In chapter 6, after spelling out the Christian's armour against the devil, he stresses the need for all believers to be constant in prayer. He

---

[103] Psalm 31:15

includes his own need for prayer that he would be given the right words 'whenever I speak'. That is a very good prayer for all of us, but particularly apt when we are prone to complaining.

Our church supports the two missionaries I mentioned in chapter 4. They work at an orphanage in South Africa with an evangelistic outreach to a local village. Three of our church members are committed to praying together for them regularly, which our friends find to be an invaluable support. A recent meeting was so often interrupted that we began to wonder whether something was going on with the work that Satan did not like. Perhaps he was trying to thwart our prayers. We accordingly prayed all the more fervently that any attack would be foiled, and our friends would be protected.

Later we checked with them to find out what had been happening at the time of our meeting. They told us that they had been in the village, telling the people about Jesus, and that three men had decided to become believers. Evidently the Holy Spirit, who had clearly nudged us to pray harder for them, had used our friends' words to convict the three of their need. During the same visit a newly-converted villager confessed to alcohol addiction. He was trying to cut back, and had come to our friends for prayer. Prayer changes things, and people too – something that Paul knew well.

Practising the presence of God. Brother Lawrence was a lay brother in a 17th century Carmelite community. A book of his writings was published posthumously, using the above title. His message was the same as that of another man of the 17th century, the English priest and poet George Herbert. In his poem *The Elixir*, he spoke of the humblest of tasks (like sweeping a room) as being done for the sake of his loving, ever-present Lord. Both of these men followed the example of Paul, who learned 'in any and every situation to be content.'[104] All three men trusted that God, who permits even adverse circumstances, would still bless them there. Complaints would have thrown doubt on the promises of God.

Centuries later we, too, should maintain the practice of remembering that God is with us whatever is happening, whether good or not so good, in the public eye or in our small corners. He has allowed it all. As we

---

[104] Philippians 4:12

learn to trust him without complaint, he will use each circumstance to fulfil his good purpose for our lives.

The peace of God is one of our most important resources for living in contentment rather than complaint. A few verses before Paul mentioned his contentment to the Philippians, he encouraged them to rejoice, and to put aside anxiety as they committed their concerns to God. Then, he said, 'the peace of God, which transcends all understanding, will guard your hearts and minds in Christ Jesus.'[105] Some of us are more prone to anxiety than others, and find it hard to let go of it. There were times when even Paul was anxious, as when he was very worried about how one of his more critical letters had been received.[106] The fact that the letter produced the desired effect in its recipients must have taught him to entrust his problems to God, and in this way to learn peace and contentment. Paul knew, because he had learned it, that whatever the demands on him, he would be given the strength he needed to surmount them.[107]

---

[105] Philippians 4:4-7
[106] 2 Corinthians 2:4; 2 Corinthians 7:8-9
[107] Philippians 4:11-13

Arriving at contentment

When things crop up in life which tempt us to be anxious and complaining, we can, like Paul, learn to commit them to our loving Lord, knowing that he will help to bring us peace of heart. In time we will realise that in all things God works for the good of those who love him.[108] He has allowed us our testing circumstances, just as he allowed Satan to inflict so much suffering in the story of faithful Job. The afflicted man emerged awestruck when he was shown the greatness of the God who could have spared him earlier but had chosen not to do so. Job's complete commitment to God whatever happened had stood the test, and his faith was strengthened by it.[109]

In lesser trials than those experienced by either Paul or Job, we too will gradually learn not to complain but to be at peace as we hold on to the fact that God has allowed our disappointment, discomfort or even disaster for his own reasons. He trusts us to trust him.

We can either obey or disobey the instruction not to grumble. Learning to exercise patience and self-

---

[108] Romans 8:28
[109] Job 1:6-12; 2:1-6

control comes from the work, and fruit, of God's Spirit within us. We may need repeated lessons before we recognise this, so God gives us plenty of them! Whatever happens, God has allowed it – and his purposes are always good.

Our loving Lord plans for our momentary troubles to contribute to our eternal glory by transforming us into the likeness of Jesus.[110] We need not be down-hearted. Instead we should thankfully and humbly remember what a wonderful goal God has ahead of us. In this we will be helped by our friends, God's written word, and prayer. I also find it helpful to think of my difficulties, both great and small, as times when the Holy Spirit does the Father's work of pruning my soul to make me more fruitful – so I should not protest when he gets out his secateurs.[111]

When other people have complaints, especially within the church, perhaps our Lord wants us to take some corrective action to put right what has provoked them. This is likely to involve deeper conversations than we have shared with them before, helping them to resolve

---

[110] 2 Corinthians 3:18; 2 Corinthians 4:16-18
[111] John 15:1-2

misunderstandings and restore the unity of the church family. A church can be seriously damaged by divisions and grumbles among its members, so they need to be prayerfully explored.

'Do not grumble' is a biblical instruction[112] but one which we too readily ignore. The writer to the Hebrews reminds us that we should throw off the sin that so easily entangles us, just as marathon runners discard anything that will slow them down. That means aligning our will to God's will. It helps us to remember how much Jesus endured without complaint before he returned to his Father, content with his finished work. To consider him each day will encourage us not to get tired and lose heart.[113]

Fatigue can bring irritable murmuring, but ahead of time we have been told the remedy. A quick SOS prayer can nip any complaint in the bud before it slips out – something that observers will notice, and perhaps ask why we don't swear or grumble. Opportunities like this to witness to the Prince of

---

[112] 1 Corinthians 10:10
[113] Hebrews 12:1-3

Peace can be among the good things that emerge from our testing times.

11. To God be the glory

As Christians, our life's work is to bring glory to God, in ways both small and great.[114] His glory is enhanced when others come to follow him through having seen evidence of his work in our lives,[115] and heard his words from our lips. Jesus said that it is out of the overflow of the heart that the mouth speaks.[116] Do our hearts overflow with a spirit of complaining, or of contentment?

A few years ago, when I was still working on call as a doctor, I tended to take evening telephone calls warily as a possible call to an emergency. I've been told that a

---

[114] 2 Thessalonians 1:11-12
[115] John 17:6,18-23
[116] Luke 6:45

doctor's voice will change audibly from curt to chatty when the caller turns out to be a dear friend rather than the call of duty. An old clergyman who was once in the room when I took a call like that must have overheard one of my cautious responses, because he suggested that as I went to answer the phone I should say to myself, 'To the glory of God.' He was echoing Paul's message to the Corinthians: '...whatever you do, do it all for the glory of God.'[117] That thought should curb any spirit of complaint.

Elsewhere in scripture, we hear the voice of wisdom calling powerfully to us:

> 'Today, if only you would hear his voice, "Do not harden your hearts..."' (Psalm 95:7-8)

> 'The fear of the Lord leads to life; then one rests content, untouched by trouble.' (Proverbs 19:23)

So may it be for us all. We have learned the theory, now for the practice

---

[117] 1 Corinthians 10:31

www.ingramcontent.com/pod-product-compliance
Lightning Source LLC
Chambersburg PA
CBHW071746080526
44588CB00013B/2165